learning to do without

poetry by stephan anstey

*Dedicated to those who suffer
with depression,
whether for a short period of time
or their entire lives
— but most especially for my mom,
who I miss every day..*

PRINT ISBN: 978-1-63821-731-2
EPUB ISBN: 978-1-63821-732-9
Printed in the United States of America

First Printing, 2021

Anstey Studios
231 Mt. Hope St
Lowell, MA 01854

Table of Contents

This collection of poetry is dedicated to people who suffer with depression, for whatever reason and to whatever degree. It is written as a gender-neutral study, exploring the myriad ways we break and hurt as we suffer loneliness, separation and loss. At times the narrator may seem more masculine or feminine, but it is generally intended to be neither.

The poems went their way through the course of a week, with approximately 7 poems for each day of the week, and it all culminates in a long surreal-narrative that deconstructs the types of things we learn do without.

The primary goal of the final poem is to braid the most fundamental elements of these things with a personality and regurgitates them with the barest snippet of a story. One could consider the name Ethyl as it relates both to an old lady, plastic or alcohol – any of the three or all of the three in any portion or combination.

Ideally, there is a tongue-in-cheek dark humor to the entirety of this book that culminates in the sick comedy inherent in these tragedies as they unfold.

freedom

Oh sparrow, that is joy,
i think, to waltz the zephyrus moments
there with only feathers and a song.

Tell me every secret, though I cannot love,
I will love you.

Oh sparrow, that is hope,
I know, to sing that prayer of rising
up to the footstools of God.

Touch my cheek, though I cannot dream,
I will dream of you.

Oh sparrow, that is faith,
I scream, to fly away, away
up into the solitary song of he is gone
alleluia, he is gone.

Speak my name, though I can not fly,
I will fly away with you.

prophecy & process

dreams become the twisted tale
broken, alert to the endless ways
nothing follows everything. a puppy
fourteen pennies, an old prostitute
with stringy blonde hair, bad eye-makeup
a bent cigarette

my grandmother crying out my name
over the din of the city, or the silence
too loud to tell which, why is there
a bear driving a volkswagon? who are those
kids on roof? why are they looking at me

the sky opens, orange, mauve,
white sneakers on my ears, thinking
about angels with plastic swords, hymns
to Shakespeare or Siddhartha - I bow
over my fat. they were my kids, why
did I not recognize them. My father
is a baby screaming from the top of a maple tree
on the common. a church bell rings
a school bell rings. a wedding ring's
gold glints.

white sneakers on my hands, running
away from the stars, a hummingbird as big as a whale
roars in. a lion head on his shoulder.

... I wake up in a cold sweat. What does nothing mean?

without the big 'g'

if there were music
perhaps i might believe
in love, but that sound
has no god in it
and those notes
were not written by
some angel of a better nature

it is a cacophony braided
from the pabulum of a small mind's poetry

if there were color
perhaps i might have faith
in love, but that painting
has no god in it
and those strokes
were not laid there by
some disciple of a holy truth

it is a thin gray silhouette splashed
across the sins of a small heart's imagination

so now i will sing
faithless and hopeless
colorless and sad

this sweet sexless sex
(with batteries) is my knotting of the gray
with my dread thread of all alone

mistakes made quietly

Thursday smells of dog shit
and rotting food, but that is not enough
of an excuse to stay in bed.

The half-written thank you card
to my aunt taunts me from the night table
but since I have no response
I turn away.

Even coffee can not cleanse me of that stench,
the air is thick with everything
I don't want anymore.

A dozen torn envelopes full of bills
sing arias to poverty, and I wish
it were so glamorous to be without

I tell my mother not to worry,
I'm fine, really I am, but she worries
because really I'm not.

I check my shoes
but nothing remains
except the stink of one misstep.

The coffee was fine,
but my stomach turned
and that was that.

pining away

Tuesday is the honesty of gray
draped over tall soft pine:
a weeping of hope from out of the shapeless void.

A short walk yields a cloak of drizzle
and the endless feeling of despair:
This cool damp endless morning is not a kiss.

Perhaps later, if the sun can burn all this away
my flesh will grow pink and tender
once again.

wishes & wings

later, when the mailman came
to the door, with nothing
for me, I noticed a sparrow
dart between the trees
and wished I were that free

I tossed the mail on the counter
and slipped into my bedroom
to cry artfully alone.

gentle voices called my name
but still, there were no passionate kisses
and my flesh was still untouched

the shape of lonely

On Monday
without a car
the first cloud
looked like a chicken
waiting for the oven

there were no kisses
skin remained skin
soul remained soul
and the sun beat down
on the masterful illusion
that alone was not alone

when the cloud was gone
I remembered that long kiss
happened on a monday too

severing a simple vow

Souls do not heal, they scar, they rip, they shatter
they stretch, they fade,
they fade

Souls do not dream, they sleep, they mutter, they weep
they rage, they fade,
they fade

Souls do not know, they feel, they hope, they need
they want, they fade
they fade
they die.

line dancing alone and broken

I hide in my room until the moon comes up
and lights the yard in tender mystic
then I slip the shackles of my threadbare depression
for the drowning freedom of a dance in the wet grass

Though somewhere someone things they love someone
every star laughs, because there is no such thing.

My feet are bare as my heart, and both beat
together in this no-where no-how no-when town
without passion of touch, only the music of want
want. want.

Though nowhere no one knows they need noone
the moon is kind and she bathes away such sins
as hope.

My arms reach with my eyes up to the raucous night
together from this no-where no-how no-when town
without lips to kiss, only the arc of this dance across gar-
den

paradise lost

I sip the coffee
through the same lips
that kissed other lips
that sipped other coffee

I struggle to forget
the taste of that fragile joy
of ephemery

When the coffee is gone,
the mug cleaned, and the sun
risen. I leave.

feeding off

A wren sings glibly
about seeds and bugs
and broken branches on nearby trees

things that matter
more than a touch
more than love

I say to him, "Yes little one
I understand,"
and toss seed
into the short grass
behind my house.

roamin' I's

---

in the closet where the pens and legal pads are kept
i stand and stare at the shelves brimming
with the implements of thought construction.

if i had thoughts, they are gone now, like a kiss.
like a god damned kiss.

it only takes 14 seconds before the tiny room
becomes a lacrimarium.

insignificant other

The only pertinent truth about cockroaches
is that they shit all over everything
and leave a terrible smell that never overpowers
as it dangles from the despair.

Skittering between the bottles of liquor
a half-dozen legs and a mindless quest
for something sweeter than nothing,
I watch them from my roost at the bar.

Just like any other lover, I suppose,
Then I kiss the lip of the shotglass -
tongueless and cold and desolate.

acrimony in acrylic

"I'm very visual,"
I sketch a body, until it forms
a whole stick figure
with all the parts that matter -
the mouth, the eyes,
the eyes, the legs, the eyes
the mouth, the arms, the eyes.

Words blister the paint
until the colors warp, "I'm very visual too,
but only because I need
the images. I can't understand
the words." They blister the tongue.

I clean the paint brush
and wait for the image to dry.

dashboard enlightenment

The road is not endless, no matter what anyone says
even if you have gas money
even if you have a map
even if you want it to be
eventually you find yourself
stopped.

I watch the sunset and drive
that way, because I can't see the end
and if I can't see it
i can pray it's not there.

It was never love, I think,
no matter what I think
it was never love
I think.

and I drive
until the darkness escapes me

despair on an unfluffed pillow

If sleep were that perfect black
without sound or thought, perhaps
i would love it.

But it neither black nor silent,
it is the voice of sorrow and disgrace
where love is how we spell regret.

I do not count the sheep
as I lay there waiting to be tortured,
I implore them to go away
and leave me to enjoy the squalor of my life
in peace.

I do not watch the clock
I glare at it as I shake delicately
between rough sheets, demanding that it move
more quickly, so the day might emancipate me
from this kissless prison

I do not take pills
as I lay there waiting for my cushy little hell,
I imagine them
and the worse hells I have not imagined
as yet. Graceful daylight will come soon ehough
I lie to myself.

wasting away behind double hung windows

outside, pine trees shuffle needles
in the whiff of a breeze, chuckling
over this oppressive heat

my bed is uncomfortable
sheets on the floor
i ruffle around myself

i imagine a squirrel sleeps
soundly in a cool nest
holed beneath an old oak root

my pillow is damp
covered in sweat
no cool spot no matter how
i adjust it

outside, an owl, like a wraith
wings between trees
silent and silver
in this forlorn moon

the shadow of my robe
dances on my closet door
slowly, as if tragedy is here

separation

---

half of my bed is empty
where my problems used to sleep

now they roam the world
and I do not know what they do
except for hate

(un)cleaned & (de)pressed

the iron is hot
but i can not afford
to strike

i am too old
too near dead
my bones ache
my heart aches

i am alone amongst
rumpled cotton
clean and fresh-seeming

but the iron is hot
and i can not afford to strike

so i press on
and on
to work.

manifestation of bitterness

The phone rings, but
i do not answer. i listen
to the voice of a stranger
explain to me the plight
of children somewhere
and an envelope they'll leave
on my door.

at my desk, i overhear a friend
explaining the scam, and i smirk
inwardly that my inner miser
and outer poverty save me
from stupidity.

Alleluia.

the shape of loss

Perhaps, that cloud that remains
is not a lizard eating an angel
the memory of a face between legs

Perhaps there was a kiss, well placed
well executed, eternally remembered

by that cloud as she slips around the world
changing the shape of her heart
as she holds on to the wide cold blues
of that dear sky

a texture of need

at bedtime, the crickets sang with their legs
about holy things like the darkness,
the stars, the clouds i can not see
but still remember

the moon pretended to wax on
philosophical about solitude

i can not accept this kissless needing
until i remember my grandfather
singing to me in a darkness like this

and i remember,
it was a Monday night
there was no kiss
other than fingers entwined
there was no touch

i can close my eyes
and need only that song

edging

I see lips, almost parted,
telling me the book that must be written
and I say,"I already know the secret."

I double-take when the sun is there again,
the honest gray has become this glaring lie
of warmth.

This sexless, dreamless, endless trek
through wakefulness to another place
where I am locked in coitus with the mirror of myself
becomes the metaphor, when before
it was simply work.

The lips whisper too softly,
I can not make out the words except,
"There are secrets left for you to know."

keeping the good china

A meal is a lonely thing, with meat and vegetables
separated, then combined by force of tooth.

There is an empty seat that rages against me
with the force years and bad sex, a hurricane
of guilt and anguish - swirling without a face
to remind me of the tussled hair in the warm sunlight
when there was still love.

Bite by bite, a sick feeling builds in a full stomach
until the meal is gone and only the emptiness remains.

cube farming

In the gentle hell of this buzzing lights
I learn the value of the waters of the river Lethe.

Paper is communion with the reckless God of money
and I count my time carefully,
perhaps they'll pay me more
if I am passionate when I recite the litany
of human resource and corporate nihility.

Hail ballpoints full of ink
doodles are with thee

In the gentle hell of these buzzing lights
I learn the values of..

it is so good to forget what I value.
Still, I miss lips entangled in lips.

salvation & repentance

Behind the couch
a Christmas ornament
spends July in meditation

until a broom
in search of a catnip mouse
pushes all that joy out into the open
to be crushed
swept up
and thrown away.

Either way,
the cat naps gracefully on the ottoman.

I start to cry as I pet her.

collating

"Why is love's loss like a staple?"
no one asks me, but I know
the answer, because my heart
bleeds from two tiny holes
and hurts as if it might never heal.

This pain, it seems, holds me
together, and if it is removed
perhaps all these pages will blow away.

"Why did I write myself in prose?"
I ask myself, because a poem
can be fit so easily upon a single sheet.

Orion and lightning bugs

a fruit bat wings along
the cotton edge of summer evening
between all the starry host above
and the starry glade below

eyes open, now, faith floods a heart
eyes open, now, hope becomes a salve
eyes open, now, love sings

a fruit bat disappears
into the mystic velvet of summer night
between the mauve hush of twilight before
and the golden silence of dawn to come

a blank stare while sitting at the kitchen table

The sound of the feet of a hundred ants
on the filthy linoleum resounds across
the kitchen like a cool breeze of desolation.

Body after body, in a thin line carrying
everything to everyone, until the thunder of tears
seems like a benediction on endless loss.

Without spray, the trek continues unabated
until everyone is full, and the puddle pulses
with a new life of broken sadness.

"Darling," echoes by the stove, "Beloved,"
by the fridge. The ants eat their fill
as their brethren carry another man's waste
to their empty dinner plates.

face in hands in shade of oak

The grackle calls, "Chewink Chewink,"
from his nasty perch into my madness
as if my despair might feed him like corn.

The iridescent blue of his face plucks
feathery jazz from the moment and holds it
ready to grow my grief into his hunger

as he flies away with an empty belly,
I realize how honest he was, and even a pest
can be more kind than love.

riverwalk

a gangly Friday morning seems more robust
before the sun can bare his bones
thus, one's ill prepared for that loss of love
that comes from another night alone

the fat of five thousand perfect stars suggests
a happy meat beside the black river
before the multitudes awake to such shame
as this angry heart-broken sliver.

Yet we do not meet, fat or skinny. I turn
away, though even the cyclone can not bend me,
to be that branch that ends without a leaf
to illustrate where brutish fate might send me

forgetting what I'm doing

A spoon becomes the center of the universe,
beneath a ceiling fan, in the left hand of an idiot,
as all thought escapes.

The spoon reflects in the cold dead eyes
of someone who has no idea what they were doing

The reflection of the spoon can not ladle love into the
belly
or catch teardrops for proper sipping.

Everything is turning on the notion that this vague loss
is not everything.

heated calamity

the water is boiled
a teabag is chosen
from the nameless faceless plethora of sameness
in that pretty green box covered in flowers

as it drops to the bottom
Darjeeling ripples outward, until
the pure becomes the memory
and the tainted becomes
the taste and the water is gone

salted chills and solitude

from the parking lot,
I hear two gulls screaming
over trash, and wonder
about the sea

the clutch of wet sand
between toes as tongues rollicked
like the hint of tide coming in
and in and in

when the scrap was gone
they flew away, neither
satisfied.

another perfect Saturday morning

My every bone practices for the grave
until the sun is halfway done with the day
because the darkness is the only thing
that can save me from an early epitaph.

My only head remains affixed to a cheap pillow
until it is betrayed by my only body
and the certain need to dispose of everything
that was once me, if only for a moment

my heart breaks. For the grave,
when the moon rises into the afternoon,
I huddle nice clothes and no shoes at all
into a pile with a short note about myself.

My fingers seem like a story I've never heard
as I tell them to grip a number two pencil
because there's just one more thing I need
to jot down for the sake of posterity.

My clothes go back gently into the night
into the drawer where clean socks rage
and there are no words. Am I the grave man
now? Cursing, blessing, dying with blind eyes?

Rehearsal is done, my bones are ready, one by one
they creak and pop and sputter into the afternoon.
There are no thoughts because there are no words
and I am frail here in this bed without deeds.

soft lips, long kisses

A dragonfly sits upon purple aster
near a guppy pond, this silence
this beauty, this is the last kiss
we should have shared before we left.

The dragonfly wings buzz briefly then
off across the glade, they play
in the July sunlight as if they forget
they were ever larva playing in a pond.

The dragon fly wings are stained glass
images, a transparent film that knows
how easily love can fly away or worse
tear apart in a sad cold wind.

The aster shuffles joy on that self-same breeze,
into the tall reeds that sidle the tea-colored water
of the little pond. The dragonfly is gone.

by the mailbox after lunch

a crack in the pavement extends
all the way to the middle of the street
like a trench protecting ants
from the crush of on-coming traffic

i look both ways then choose
not to cross. I step on the crack
turn back and start to cry
but it's not for the ants
they're fine. they're all fine.

without

cash money on the hutch
in a small pile
worth next to nothing

next to nothing, and
a crystal snifter
without any brandy

i think, next to nothing
standing next to nothing
with next to nothing

i wonder how I'll do without
brandy? I find the ice
and the Wild Turkey

"Gobble, gobble," i sneer
take a long draught
of that hard cold bird

and feel next to nothing.

memory of a touch

It is a sunless sun that only burns
but does not warm, like every kiss
we ever shared.

Under the crab apple tree
eleven children play game-less games
that only warm
but never burn,
like heaven without a kiss.

Their shadows twist around their feet
like jump ropes, but they do not trip.
their voices knot their joy around my stomach
until it asphyxiates my hope

the sun, the damned sun, fingers our flesh
until the tickle of my loneliness
can not be distinguished from the long rays
of a perfect summer afternoon
dancing in a sprinkler in cut-offs and camp t-shirts.

staring into the darkness alone

If there is such a thing as joy
it is the intangible thing
that feels cool and damp
as my hands reach out
then warm and dry as my tears
reach down. I remain
unconvinced in this
and Santa Claus. The disappointment
is a raw real thing that loves me
like a cheese grater over bare knuckles
and joy does not bleed.

If there is such a thing as joy,
then it is a cruel hipster
in round wire-framed shades
rhyming about summer and sex
but never meaning love any
more than a shark means hunger. I remain
unconvinced in this
and Heaven. This disappointment
is a soft empty thing that loves me
like the heel of a new shoe over a new blister
and joy does not burst.

belching out terms of refreshment

I think of you when the ice cube snaps as it hits
the tepid tonic. Love is the same as that,
and I drink it down until my belly is full.

I get three more ice cubes, and fill the glass
again with lukewarm fizz. I drop the first two cubes
and enjoy the way they break. But not the last

I want for that. I want too long. When I drop that one
there is no snap.

Passionate Apathy

I feel absolutely nothing
when I fall asleep on a busted mattress
except the sharp hurt of a missprung spring

Was it really that long ago
when a kiss seemed real? When a kiss seemed
to linger on the edge of my morning
like the sweetness of a doughnut
as I sipped coffee?

I feel absolutely nothing
when I buy another cup to sip.

Anger is such a thin screen,
this is all so strong
and black, the cream does not rise.
Perhaps I should not rise either.

Was it really that hot
when our touch was real? When our touch seemed
so urgent, like a warm dinner after a long day
begging the rich to share
what little they have.

I feel absolutely nothing
when I wash my brown hair.

Happiness is such a pleasant lie,
this is all so kind. Truth would be kinder
if I cared.

Perhaps if I were kinder, I'd want to
care.

Snippy, Snarky, Snide
& the other depressed dwarfs

a few children, probably mine,
whirl about in the dark place
full of sunlight and music
where I hate laughter most

they eat sweet sticky things
call out to me with smiles
dance on the soft part of the grass
and lecture each other on the art
of sharing.

a few moments later, probably forever,
i spin about near the light place
full of shadow and mosquitoes
where they love me most

i eat nothing
fade out
stop
and lecture them on the art
of silence.

meditation on a bit of rice

suppose a mouse is searching the endless expanse
of some utterly immaculate linoleum kitchen floor
for some tiny scrap of nothing you dropped there
a day or two ago - but not much more - and also
suppose that somewhere a cat is hungry thinking
of a mouse searching the kitchen floor for some
tiny scrap of nothing someone dropped somewhere
recently enough to be appealing - and then, can
you suppose that the two will never realize how
they both exist in the same house at the same time

suppose you are searching everywhere but the floor
for some tiny thought you lost somewhere about
something more meaningful than food and you feel
more empty than the cat or the mouse, and like
the mouse, there is no hope of finding it, and
like the cat you have absolutely nothing
to fear except ignorance.

Good News

Sunday comes naked and Godless,
singing alone in the garden
as if the lilies may care.

If there were a book, it might be good,
or it might be nothing
but a sick fantasy full of gentiles
and miracles, but there is no bench
upon which to read it.

The lilies stand and wait for the sun
to pass. This is not the story
of a miracle, the sun will come again.

Sunday leaves like a prayer
answered only by Monday
and a sad yearning for something good

wasting away

One worm becomes two worms
as the knife slices life
in two. One worm becomes
food for the fat young hornpout
in the clear cool flow of the old brook.

But there is time, a long hot time
beneath a willow, whistling
into the Cat-o-nine-tails
and wondering about that fishercat
last night.

A hook might hurt, a tooth might hurt,
but time, that is the real agony

a lazy Sunday morning kiss

coffee steams lonely on the table
the blue napkin beside it, reminds me
there is laundry to do and
no one to help.

eggs in the fridge are chill
and ready for frying, but I have no
ambition

only plenty
of butter, salt, pepper, bacon,
sausage, sugar, syrup, milk, juice
pancake mix.

I watch the steam rise
from the coffee, and I am lonely
at the table. I pick up the napkin
to wipe my lips.

the depravity of being alone
on a Sunday night

on the corner by the convenience store
i see three monkeys lined up, scruffy
and pathetic. they need showers,
the one with coke-bottle glasses pounds
on a bucket,"Hey mister, can't ya spare
a buck?" while the one wearing the knit hat
with ear muffs sings tunelessly.

the last little monkey looks saddest of all
as she strums. her lips move in time
but no words fall out.

when i come out with 2% milk,
i see them rolling off on skateboards
filthy and pathetic,

just like me.

coping with a new future

Abject terror and unmitigated joy
eat away at the lining of the stomach
then burst forth from the bowels like
a million worms as I am reminded
of all the things I do not have.

I watch my dinner grow cold, my hands
grow cold, my heart
grow cold. I watch my face mirrored in the pane
of glass that looks out on my backyard
where the young doe chews my un-mowed grass
and wonder if want is as good as have.

The sparrow swoops down, then flies off.

This is everything
I believe.

Learning to do without

Life is composed of eleventy three things
all named ethyl, all endless, all meaning
less than the one before. Divorcing one
from the other is expensive, and
(in the event that there is such a thing) soul draining.

i.

Ethyl calcium Von Stubenstein
eats bones and marrow
eats stones and stacks them
in small piles, as if to mark territory

She draws wells
and uses the water
to clean brushes she doesn't own
to paint the stones
with neolithic quarry
she would not stalk.

On Sundays, she goes to church
to prey on the mind of a priest
in hopes his philosophy might be enough
to enlighten her on the feeling
of that universal thing she wishes
were God.

ii.

Ethyl Potassium Ichbeininberg eats smelly cheeses
and calls out to her dead husband when she sleeps.

Without her, there is no reaction.
There is no pull, no sneeze, no push,
no bending over and close examination of the rush
to judgment little boys make about 12-year-old girls
who pre-maturely develop.

With her, the sun rises, and everything else is uncertain.

iii.

Ethyl Helium Twofeather's father Sam
caught a bald eagle from the air with his bare hands
and broke both legs when he landed.

She was lighter, more lithe, and less
honest. She stole his turquoise necklace and ran off
to Houston with a boy long on hard love
short on sharp tender wit.

When she thought of God,
it was on her back, distracted
by the passion.

iv.

Ethyl Golda Biltong saved Germany from the Swedes
or something, but she didn't wear clothes
and this was enough of a problem
that her father sent her off
to the farm where cows were salted and dried.

She only laughed, and let her skin brown. She only
laughed
and let the lesions grow. She only laughed and laughed
and laughed
and died on a Wednesday at quarter past three.

Her father seemed sad, as he buried her nude body
in the family plot under a rosy stone with an angel carved
neatly
in the top left corner.

v.

Ethyl Hydrogen Quackenbush was a singular woman
with tall gray hair and no one who loved her.

She wore tall black shoes, and a short skirt
and said nothing when a parade passed.

She liked elephants, cookbooks and solar calculators
and hated that she never had anyone to play scrabble
with
late at night when she could not sleep.

vi.

Ethyl Oxygen Zachariah is covered in scars
from chicken pox when she was three. She looks
in a mirror and sees no one at all. Just like everyone else

when she writes poetry, she wishes
it was read and loved.

She wears red, mostly, and eats chicken livers
with bacon and onions and a small iced tea.

Her mind might have an original thought
someday.

vii.

Ethyl Beryllium Van Pupil extracts vanilla beans from a
leather pouch,
cracks them open, and pushes the black seed into a pile.
The smell is delightful
and no one notices that she is crying.

When she is finished, she washes it all down the sink.

The delicious odor fades away, and she forgets about her
baby girl
her baby girl who drowned.

viii.

Ethyl Ruthenium Clack sat for 3 days in a dark room
shitting on herself and thinking she was dead.

The men who carried her fat body out on a stretcher
puked twice each, and marveled that she had not died
from dehydration.

Her brother visits her twice a month
in the county hospital. He brings her black-eyed suzies
for her great grandmother's green vase.

He tells her stories of all the things they had
and when he leaves she plucks each petal, drops it on
the ground
and whispers, "He loves me not"

ix.

Ethyl Xenon Gaunt sips red sangria on the patio
as the world moves by. She almost speaks,
almost reaches out, almost
but never quite.

Her neighbor's son Mark forgets she is there
when he smokes, forgets she's there as he sips Schlitz,
forgets she's there.

The milkman does not care either way
and leaves 6 fresh upon her stoop
without a grin or hello.

x.

Ethyl Caesium Mardeux found her father's nudie
magazines
and loved him more. She thought of him fondly
years later as a man but told no one.

She dusts his picture on the mantle every day
twice and smiles, not because she is nude
but because the sunlight plays on the hardwood.

Sometimes, the hummingbird buzzes outside the window
and she wishes for something more.

xi.

Ethyl Phosphorus Rodriguez wears a floral blouse
and sings the song about the daisies
on the mountainside
her grandmother taught her
when she summered with her.

The tune dies in the ears of a cricket whose legs are tired
from his own tuneless song.

Every evening, she feeds her grandmother gruel
and cries
when she does not know her name.

"I am Ethyl, grandmother, I am Ethyl,"
she says.

"That's nice dear," her grandmother pats her arm.

xii.

Ethyl Manganese Wu tears little-faceless-man-shapes
from yesterday's newspaper and burns them in her Frank-
lin stove.

She tells stories to the wallpaper and asks,
"Did I tell you this one before?"

No one ever answers, "yes."
So she goes on.

xiii.

Ethyl Neon Zimmerman farts and pretends
it was not her. No one says a word because
she is not there. She is never there.

This is what it is to be a ghost, she thinks
but does not say. This is what it is to be
forgotten, she knows, but does not believe.

When the last of the coffee is gone, she sighs
and types away at her desk. No one remembers
to tell her it is time to go home. It is time
to go home. This is what it is to be a ghost.

xiv.

Ethyl Silver Lacrissio has cramps and lays in bed
until half-past lunch. The heating pad does not help
and outside the sunlight seems to remember
a summer day when she served tea to porcelain dolls
and sang all the air from the depths of her lungs.

She hurts. She hurts and hurts and hurts
until she bleeds. Then she hurts some more.

xv.

Ethyl Technetium Bartholomew delivered pizzas
to homeless toothless nameless men
until last week.

Now she sits in a white room screaming
at the whiteness of the white and non-existent
bugs crawling on her bloody nail-ripped flesh.

Mike Tousignant asks where Ethyl is
when Barry the fat pimply bastard
brings the pepperoni with extra cheese.

"She's not feeling well," Barry says,
and it's true enough.

xvi.

Ethyl Platinum Wurzinski dances around her kitchen
with a plum in her left hand. There is no music,
and she is afraid to take that first bite.

What if she falls as she chews, what if she falls
if she swallows, what if she has to stop dancing?

It was so much easier when the music played,
she thinks, and she wishes, oh God, how she wishes.

xvii.

Ethyl Antimony Gregory drinks green tea
alone at the oak table her uncle Albert made
in 1897. She is not dead, nor quite alive,
which he had said might happen
if she did not have children.

She hates him now, more each day,
as the table seems increasingly

perfect.

When the green tea is gone, she rises,
she rises
she rises and washes the china cup
in the warm soapy water,
stows it in the hutch and
sits down to knit a blanket
for her niece Elsa's baby Albert.

xviii.

Ethyl Plumbum Nuremburg splatters paint across canvas
cold and alone in her ex-husband's studio.

Her art ruins his, and this is not enough.

Once there were kisses, so many damned kisses
her lips were raw. Her lips were swollen. Her lips
wandered and measured love in joyful pain.

Her art dries, and this is not beautiful.

Once there were kisses, long thin kisses
that ranged the miles of body that extended passion
to the horizon. Her lips were the vehicle that carried
love from diner to diner with a smile. Her lips were the
gateway
for all the food that nourished her soul. Her lips
wandered.

Her art splashes over his, and this is not enough.

xix.

Ethyl Flourine Parker has perfect teeth. She eats
thick steak. She rends the flesh from the fork with ferocity
then digests the violence.

It is a tragedy when she chips a tooth on the fork.

She barks at the waitress, as if it is best to ascribe blame
to the innocent than accept it on one's own sad sick soul.

It is a tragedy when the waitress cries,
but no one realizes this is how the world ends.

xx.

Ethyl Ununtrium Dunkirk imagines a purpose
beyond boiling water for spaghetti
as her baby bawls beside her.

Her husband Dan imagines her sister Arlene naked
in his arms, unaware that she hates him
and his God-damned crying baby,
if hate is even possible in a heart that does not care.

There was a time when nudity was good,
and their purpose
was so bare before them that every detail bore their
identity
like a stamp of legitimacy.

She likes it best Al dente, but that crispness is gone.

The naked truth is such a soft corpulent thing.

Epilog

without love, without dreams,
without hope, without food,
without future, without touch,
without money, without art,
without history, without sex,
without want, without purpose

Life is still life.

This is the quietly unassuming
agonizing element every Ethyl knows
as she cries & cries & cries & cries …

About the Author

Stephan Anstey is a poet, and artist. He is a member of Lowell Poetry Network, The Arts League of Lowell and the founder of the Lowell Writers Group. With his beloved and most assuredly to-be-sainted wife of more than 25 years Ellen, he lives in the historic mill city of Lowell, Massachusetts. Stephan is most inspired by his two children, Emily and Cameron, as well as the rest of his extremely large family and circle of friends. He loves to closely examine the uncertain edges of our common humanity, where all the definitions of things are too fuzzy to be sure. His poetry has been featured in many poetry blogs, several print journals including the Lowell Offering, and can be found daily on Anstey.org, Facebook, Twitter, and all the other places people congregate online.